A
PRAYER
JOURNEY
THROUGH
DEPLOYMENT

A PRAYER JOURNEY THROUGH DEPLOYMENT

THE PRAYERS OF A MOM

DONNA MULL

Pleasant Word
A Division of WinePress Group

CONTENTS

PROLOGUE

Nothing motivates us more in life than love and pain. When my son received his orders for deployment to Iraq, I was motivated by both. I had heard stories about mothers whose faithful prayers had changed lives. I wanted to be one of those mothers. Initially, I sought out a prayer support group of other families in my church who might be facing the same burden. At the time there was only one. To enlist the prayers of more people, I decided to write weekly prayer devotionals that focused on specific prayer needs of soldiers and their families and send them to friends and family as a springboard for their own prayers. As recipients forwarded the devotionals to others, the contact list grew. What follows is a year-long journey of prayer. Because God's Word is timeless and universally relevant, these Scripture-based prayers often spoke to non-military people engaged in various battles of their own. May they speak to you and give expression to the cry of your heart.

Our journey began in June and ended a year later in June. Every journey is defined by the day to day experiences that happen along the way—national events, holidays, deaths, and many others. Your journey may begin on a different calendar date and will be unique to your own experiences. Whether you read this book as a chronological journey, select a topic from the table of contents that speaks to your need, or jump ahead to a holiday that comes at a different point in your journey, my prayer is that you will see God walking with you every step of the way.

—Donna Mull
June 2009

LONELINESS

The LORD God said, "It is not good for the man to be alone."

—Genesis 2:18

God sets the lonely in families.

—Psalm 68:6

But Jesus often withdrew to lonely places and prayed.

—Luke 5:16

Father, after creating all things and proclaiming them good, you found one thing that was not good—for man to be alone.

God of relationship—Father, Son, and Holy Spirit: enjoying perfect harmony and unity from eternity past, you desired that we would have relationship with you and with each other. Indeed, it is the most heartfelt need of all of us. For those of us surrounded by family, friends, and familiar surroundings, it is hard to even imagine what it feels like to be a soldier, far from home in a hostile place, or to be a family member who so desperately misses their loved one.

Tender God who created a helper for Adam and *set the lonely in families*, will you provide the sense of relationship the human soul so desperately needs? Help soldiers to become family to one another. May we, as extended family, friends, and neighbors, reach out in tangible ways and be faithful to pray for the soldier families all around us. Enlarge our hearts to care deeply and serve them in any way we can.

Father, may every lonely soldier and family member find what Jesus found in you when he walked on earth: a constant consciousness of your love and presence that takes away the pain of loneliness. In your great mercy, fill the terrible void in their hearts that they are powerless to fill. Draw each one near to your heart and comfort them.

In Jesus' name, Amen.

MISSION

"My food," said Jesus, "is to do the will of him who sent me and to finish his work."

—John 4:34

One of the most evident features of Christ's life was his singleness of purpose, his clarity of mission. It defined his actions, fueled his passion, and enabled him to endure unimaginable suffering and stress. He knew why he had come and what he had to do. He knew the end result that would make every sacrifice worth the cost.

Father, my heart aches for our soldiers caught in the tension of unclear purposes and stark divisions of support in the homeland that sent them. They fight an enemy that is not easily recognized by uniform and weapon. The rules of engagement are gray. The enemy could be a woman in a crowded market place or a young child who is trained to hate. Guide them with your wisdom. Grant them discernment. I pray that they might offer this service up to you so that it will take on the significance of a heavenly mission that has purposes that transcend earth.

May clarity of mission come from you. War confronts soldiers with those invisible realities that define life. Knowing what they believe, value, and live for suddenly becomes very important. One marine, speaking of his dead comrade, says it poignantly:

[He] went in an instant. I probably will, too. But I wish I knew something about what's on the other side. I wish I believed something or I had done something that makes it all worthwhile. I hate the thought of dying, but I hate the thought of dying empty most of all.[1]

Father, I earnestly pray that every soldier and family member here at home will have the certainty that their sacrifices are not empty. I pray that no soldier's faith needs will go unmet. Equip chaplains to help soldiers who grapple with the questions of war and what waits for them on the other side. Strengthen each soldier's grasp on invisible realities. Do so for their families as well. May our soldiers be guided by a code of conduct whose author is neither man nor government.

In Jesus' name, Amen.

FEAR

"Do not let your hearts be troubled. Trust in God; trust also in me."

—John 14:1

Then Jesus went about a stone's throw away from them. He kneeled down and prayed, "Father, if you are willing, take away this cup of suffering. But do what you want, not what I want." Then an angel of heaven appeared to him to strengthen him. Being full of pain, Jesus prayed even harder. His sweat was like drops of blood falling to the ground.

—Luke 22:41-44 NCV

A just-*God* Jesus could make us but not understand us. A just-*man* Jesus could love us but never save us. But a *God-man* Jesus? Near enough to touch. Strong enough to trust. (emphasis mine)[2]

Thank you, Jesus, that you are a God-man. We need a God who understands what we feel. The fact that you felt fear when the suffering of the cross loomed over you and told us about it gives us freedom to do the same. There was no pretense of strength—only a request. I am relieved that we do not have to be strong, just real. Jesus, you brought your fears right to the Father, just as your Word tells us to do: "When I am afraid, I will put my trust in you" (Ps. 56:3).

Today, Father, for ourselves and our deployed loved ones, we do the same. No masks, no bravado—just our anxious fears.

Will our soldier loved ones be OK? Will we? Will they have the strength to get through this? Will we? Will they come back the same person we kissed goodbye? Who will we be?

And now we do what Jesus did: we cry out to you. May our soldiers feel the liberty to do the same, and know that you will understand. When anxieties and cares press down on us and threaten to poison our inner lives, help us find our peace in you. God-man, strong enough to save and near enough to touch, bring this deployment to a good ending. We need your reassuring touch, and we pray for your mighty power to protect and save.

Offered up after the example of Christ, Amen.

DEPLOYED

O God, our help in ages past, Our hope for years to come,
Our shelter from the stormy blast, And our eternal home!
Under the shadow of Thy throne Still may we dwell secure;
Sufficient is Thine arm alone, And our defense is sure.
—Hymn by Isaac Watts, 1674-1748

I went to the Fourth of July parade feeling the need to
applaud a soldier. I was a spectator, like I had been in other
years, but now it was personal. There, in the midst of the parade,
I saw the raw material for my prayer: a group of military wives
marching in front of their husbands' National Guard unit.
They were wearing T-shirts. On the front, their shirts read:
"When a soldier serves," and on the back, they read: "So does
the family." One woman marched backwards so that the rest of
the message would not be missed.

That truth compels me to pray for families. Who prepares
them for deployment? No "theater immersion training" for
them prior to their loved one's tour of duty. Is being prepared
even possible? I hardly know how to pray for them except come
to them in their point of need.

Father, come in the divine, doing what only God can do.
Come in the human, compelling friends, neighbors, family,
and even strangers to fulfill the needs that are within their
ability to fulfill. Come as a tender father to children missing
their parents. Come as a compassionate friend to lonely and
overwhelmed spouses. Come as a counselor in moments of
difficult decisions. Come as a healer when hearts are hurting.

Come as a source of hope and strength when they are at their wits' end. Be all in all to them.

In the Savior's name, Amen.

DESERT LESSONS— GUIDANCE AND PROTECTION

By day the LORD went ahead of them in a pillar of cloud to guide them on their way and by night in a pillar of fire to give them light, so that they could travel by day or night. Neither the pillar of cloud by day nor the pillar of fire by night left its place in front of the people.

—Exodus 13:21-22

Jesus Christ is the same yesterday and today and forever.

—Hebrews 13:8

Father, as I think of my son headed for deployment in a desert land, I am drawn to the lessons immersed in the history of Israel's forty-year wanderings. The pillar of cloud and fire specifically met the unique needs of their wanderings. It led them through a trackless wasteland, like a GPS in a land without maps or road signs. It shielded them from the scorching desert heat that would have quickly claimed their lives. It gave light to their darkness, both the literal darkness of night and the figurative darkness of not knowing where to go next. You have always come to us in the shape and form of our need, Lord. We are often unaware or slow to recognize your presence, but Israel couldn't have missed it!

Changeless God, be to our soldier loved ones and to us *the same yesterday and today and forever*. Guide, shield, and light our way in whatever manifestation we need. Guide our thoughts, attitudes, and actions through the dark places of ignorance, worry, confusion, and depression that we may encounter in this foreign, harsh, and unfamiliar desert. Give us light for the next step when we cannot see where to place our foot. Build in us the trust of daily dependence on you.

In the name of Jesus, who called himself *the light of the world*, Amen.

DESERT LESSONS—PROVISION

Then the LORD said to Moses, "I will rain down bread from heaven for you. The people are to go out each day and gather enough for that day. In this way I will test them and see whether they will follow my instructions."
—Exodus 16:4

Then Moses said to them, "No one is to keep any of it until morning." . . . Each morning everyone gathered as much as he needed, and when the sun grew hot, it melted away.
—Exodus 16:19, 21

Father, teach us how to apply this truth in the present situation. We must deal with deployment one day at a time. There is nothing we can bank or store up. Today's strength will not cover tomorrow. Today's calm will not see us through tomorrow's crisis. Military strategy and experience cannot protect us from the unknowns behind the next door. Like the manna that had to be collected every day in proportion to that day's need, we still need to depend on you for day-to-day provision. I pray that we will *pass the test* and follow your instruction, whether we are soldier or family.

The provision was your part; the gathering was the people's. Supply matched need.

There are so many layers of meaning here, Lord. Provide for the physical needs of our soldiers: nourishment, rest, stamina, health, shelter, and safety. Provide for their emotional needs as well: wisdom, discernment, clarity of purpose, courage, guidance, and peace. And most importantly, fulfill their spiritual needs: the knowledge of your presence, assurance of your care of loved ones, and confidence in their eternal safety.

And what about the *gathering* part? How do you gather when the bullets are flying? May it be in their constant state of mind to step out in faith and daily dependence on you, Jesus, *the bread of heaven.*

Amen.

RESILIENCE

"I am the vine; you are the branches. If a man remains in me and I in him, he will bear much fruit; apart from me you can do nothing."

—John 15:5

With a soldier loved one headed for a combat-torn country, I see parables where I did not notice them before. Recently, a swift moving brush fire swept through the coastal vegetation near my home, threatening nearby homes and leaving a swath of charred earth in its wake. The landscape was completely altered. I will never forget the swarms of screaming birds flying chaotically over what had been their safe and familiar home just minutes before. Against the backdrop of the bay stood the charred skeletons of trees that had been on the verge of bursting into the vibrant colors of spring. The direction of the wind spared human dwellings, by forcing the fire towards the water.

How like this fire are the unexpected fires of life that sweep upon us? We go along anticipating and expecting the vibrant life of spring, and then a deployment order comes, or a letter, or a diagnosis, and the landscape is completely changed. We chaotically search for what was comfortable, safe, and familiar. That is certainly not unique to military life; perhaps we just think about it more when we have deployed loved ones.

But, interestingly, the effects of the fire are the heart of the parable. Things were *uncovered* by the fire. The original marsh lands had been overrun by an invasive tall marsh grass, because three broken down culverts had blocked the flow of salt water that was essential to the health of the ecosystem. With the cause now visible, correction and restoration was possible. With amazing speed, black was replaced with green, and new growth began to cover the wounded earth. Some of those charred skeletons of trees now have tufts of green leaves pushing out of the blackened, seemingly dead branches near the trunk. Life is resilient. But the new leaves did not grow on the periphery—only near the trunk and its supply of life giving sap.

Father, as a soldier's mom, I feel compelled to pray: PREVENT the life fires from sweeping into the lives of deployed soldiers and their families. But if the fire comes, direct the course of the wind to avert human tragedy. If the fire comes, may it be a controlled burn, whose boundaries are determined by your sovereign and loving hand. If the fire comes, may what it uncovers lead to perfect restoration. If the fire comes, may it burn off the invasive grasses that have choked out the true life you intended. Let the end result be strong and vibrant life. Help each soldier and family member trust you to provide and keep them safe when comfortable and familiar territory cannot be found. And keep them always close to the source of life so that nothing they experience can suppress the resilient life within.

In Jesus' name, Amen.

ARMED

For now we see in a mirror, dimly. . . .
> —1Corinthians13:12 NKJV

But we prayed to our God and posted a guard day and night. . . . After I looked things over, I stood up and said to the nobles, the officials and the rest of the people, "Don't be afraid of them. Remember the Lord, who is great and awesome. . . ." From that day on, half of my men did the work. . . . Those who carried materials did their work with one hand and held a weapon in the other. . . .
> —Nehemiah 4: 9, 14, 16, 17

For the weapons of our warfare are not carnal but mighty in God for pulling down strongholds.
> —2 Corinthians 10:4 NKJV

As I ponder the difficult questions of war, I feel as though I am looking in a mirror dimly. Nothing is clear to me, not even the things I think I see that are biased by my own feelings, experiences, and sources of information. So I look to you, God.

Reveal your redeeming purposes in this war. War is as old as mankind. The Bible is dotted with stories of war, yet you always worked in the midst of it. My prayers are formed from your very own Word.

In the story of Nehemiah and his men, surrounded by enemies, obeying your call to rebuild the wall of Jerusalem, two actions stand out: *He prayed and then looked things over, and his men did the work of rebuilding with one hand while with the other they held a weapon.*

Prayer is the starting point, Lord. I pray for your will and direction for our soldiers. Give military leaders the wisdom and discernment to look things over carefully before recommending action. I pray that this whole involvement will be as much about rebuilding as defending. Let the eye of every soldier see what needs to be done to help the nation rebuild, and lend willing hands to the process. At the same time, keep them always alert and vigilant to the enemy's efforts to prevent rebuilding.

I pray that our soldiers will bear the kind of weapons that are mighty for pulling down generations-deep strongholds of hatred, oppression, and distrust. Give soldiers your love for the people. May they be instruments of healing and reconciliation as they help the nation rebuild. Let integrity be the foundation of all they do as they are the face of America to the world. May they lead by honorable example. Let justice be done as seen through the eyes of God, who alone sees all things. May victory be measured in acts of kindness and compassion that are done in humility and love—like the victory of the Cross.

In Jesus' name, Amen.

SACRIFICE

> Then I heard the voice of the Lord saying, "Whom shall I send? And who will go for us?" And I said, "Here am I. Send me!"
>
> —Isaiah 6:8

From the moment I shared the first prayer in this book, my intent has been to pray for *all* deployed soldiers and their families—though I hold a particular one in preeminence in my heart. Today, God, it seemed as though you personalized it so. I can only pray from my own heart and ask you to divinely edit it for each intended heart. Just days from when I know my son will board a plane for Iraq, you had me revisit a poignant, tender, joyful memory: my son's wedding.

The offertory music at today's church service was the Twila Paris song, "How Beautiful," done in a very moving way with soft guitar music, images on a screen, and a dramatic reading of the lyrics. This song was beautifully sung at my son and daughter-in-law's wedding. It is a love song, but of a love that is light years above romantic love. It is a story of sacrificial love *and of hands that serve.* As I listened to this song, all hope of keeping my composure crumbled. I wept as I thought of how you have brought this couple full circle to this place of sacrificial love. I pray that you bless the sacrifice and those who make it. Bless the heart willing to be sent. Bless the heart that allows the soldier to go. May they both exemplify Christ in this sending. May my son, by the conduct of his life, be a light in a dark place and the expression of your love where people so desperately need it.

In Jesus' name, Amen.

VULNERABLE

People were bringing little children to Jesus to have him touch them, but the disciples rebuked them. When Jesus saw this, he was indignant. He said to them, "Let the little children come to me, and do not hinder them, for the kingdom of God belongs to such as these." . . . And he took the children in his arms, put his hands on them and blessed them.

—Mark 10:13-14, 16

A father to the fatherless, a defender of widows, is God in his holy dwelling.

—Psalm 68:5

Jesus, your protective, tender love for children is unmistakable in Scripture. You used their trusting innocence as an object lesson and gave strong warning to anyone who would cause them harm. You even called yourself *father* to the fatherless. Much of this world's sorrow falls upon the shoulders of children, so vulnerable and unequipped to handle it. Certainly it is so for children of deployed soldiers. *All* children need the love, nurture, protection, guidance, modeling, and discipline of their parents to equip them for life, and when a parent is deployed, their children share the cost.

I pray for these children. Take them into your arms and be their father or mother while their parents are absent. Bring good and godly people into their lives who will act as role models, teachers, wise counselors, tender nurturers, comforters,

19

protectors, and faithful friends. Give sensitivity to all who may touch their lives. The losses soldiers' kids experience are worthy of grief, and for some the process is harder than others. For some, it occurs during strategic times in their development. Give wisdom and compassion to those who stand in the gap while a parent is away. Provide the discipline and boundaries necessary to prevent compounding sorrow. May we learn from the disciples' error and intentionally bring the children to Jesus for blessing—in prayer, and perhaps literally, by taking them with us to church, or helping them access the resources of faith.

Your ways are not ours, Lord. We would shelter ourselves and our children from every painful thing, but your way is to take the painful thing and use it as a tool to fashion something good. I pray that you redeem the pain that soldiers' children experience. Use it to make them strong, wise, compassionate, and unselfish servants who may change their world in their own time and way. Protect their tender spirits from cynicism, bitterness, and depression. Preserve in them that wonderful, resilient, trusting, exuberant, full-of-life spirit. By your grace, may that be what we model for them.

In Jesus' name, Amen.

CARED FOR

"Look at the birds in the sky! They don't plant or harvest. They don't even store grain in barns. Yet your Father in heaven takes care of them. Aren't you worth more than birds?"

—Matthew 6:26 CEV

Careless in the care of God. And why shouldn't they be?
For their food, He provides insects in the air,
seeds on the ground.
For their search for food, He provides eyes that are keen,
wings that are swift.
For their drinking, He provides poolings of rainwater.
For their bathing, He provides puddles.
For their survival, He provides migratory instincts to take
them to warmer climates.
For their flight, He provides bones that are porous and
lightweight.
For their warmth, He provides feathers.
For their dryness, He provides a water-resistant coating.
For their rest, He provides warm updrafts so they can glide
through the air.
For their journey, He provides the company of other
travelers.
For their return, He provides the companionship of a
mate.
For their safety, He provides a perch in branches far from
the reach of predators.
For their nest, He provides twigs.

21

And for every newborn beak, He provides enough worms
so they can grow up to leave the nest and continue the
cycle of life.
It's no wonder they're so free from the cares of this world.
The wonder is, if we count more to Him than birds, why
aren't we?

—Ken Gire[3]

Grant unto us, almighty God, the peace of God that
passeth understanding,
That we, amid the storms and troubles of this our life, may
rest in thee,
knowing that all things are in thee;
Not beneath thine eye only, but under thy care,
governed by thy will, guarded by thy love,
So that with a quiet heart we may see the storms of life,
the cloud and the thick darkness,
Ever rejoicing to know that the darkness and the light are
both alike to thee. . . .

—George Dawson[4]

Father, thank you for the anointed words of others that
speak to our concerns and articulate our deepest prayers better
than we ever could ourselves. Thank you that our soldiers and
their families are under the watchful care of the Almighty. You
have anticipated all of their needs, and you will provide. When
the darkness creeps in, help us find our peace in remembering
who you are.

In Jesus' name, Amen.

UNITY

"I want all of them to be one with each other, just as I am one with you and you are one with me."

—John 17:21 CEV

The body is a unit, though it is made up of many parts; and though all its parts are many, they form one body. . . . If they were all one part, where would the body be?. . . If one part suffers, every part suffers with it; if one part is honored, every part rejoices with it.

—1 Corinthians 12:12, 19, 26

Many elements of modern life, such as busyness, technology, materialism, and divergent views, seem to isolate and separate us from the world. A generation of young people is growing up with minimal skills of human connectedness, and their parents are finding connectedness more a memory than a reality. As a nation, we are as divided as we have ever been. It is here, perhaps, that the military has a lesson for us all.

Soldiers come together from every walk of life: as scholars, doctors, executives, chaplains, mechanics, computer technicians, and more. Their personalities are as diverse as the stars in the sky. They are a blend of races and cultures. Their beliefs, values, opinions, and political persuasions diverge. And yet, when they come together like many tributaries into one great river of mission, they are one in purpose, aim, and spirit—not uniform, but united, transcending their differences through a common focus. All of their privileges, possessions, preoccupations, and personal pursuits have been stripped away. The fragility of life becomes a solemn reality and interdependence becomes essential to survival. What would the world be like if our nation, the church, or even families could do the same?

Lord God, in tense and pressured moments, when tempers flare and fears erupt, help soldiers make the sacrifices necessary for the greater purpose to be achieved. Like parts of the human body that contribute something essential to the body's health and function, let each soldier's contribution be valued. Father, may the experience of unity be etched in the soldiers' hearts, that they may come home and teach us. Let the witness of their unity be a powerful influence in nations where ethnic divisions are stark and volatile. As a nation, help us to redefine the foundational, enduring values that made us a blessed nation and seek unity in them. Father, I do not think this is even possible apart from you. Give us your spirit of unity.

Amen.

LOSS

"Blessed are those who mourn, for they will be comforted."
—Matthew 5:4

The Spirit of the Sovereign LORD is on me, because the LORD has anointed me. . . . He has sent me to bind up the brokenhearted . . . to comfort all who mourn . . . and provide for those who grieve in Zion—to bestow on them a crown of beauty instead of ashes, the oil of gladness instead of mourning, and a garment of praise instead of a spirit of despair.

—Isaiah 61:1, 2, 3

This week we will revisit the memory of that awful day in our history when all of life stood still—the attack of September 11, when life was tragically cut short for so many Americans. To live is to know loss, for loss touches every human life. Whether it is swift and merciless like the events of September 11, changing our lives in a moment, or slow like erosion, imperceptibly wearing away at something that seemed so strong and sure, loss can be individual and isolating or national and uniting. It is not something we would ever volunteer to experience, but it shows up like an uninvited guest.

Soldiers and military families are deeply acquainted with loss. Some have known the ultimate loss of life itself. Many have lost health, limbs, function, and soundness of mind. Some lose careers, and some lose marriages. But *all* lose precious time with loved ones that cannot be regained, such as milestone events in children's lives, day-to-day conversations and encounters with a spouse that feed the soul, the sharing of life's joys and burdens, and the spending of precious time with aging parents. Soldiers lose the freedom to choose how they spend their time.

Lord, comfort soldiers and their families whose losses are both great and small. Bless them for the sacrifices they make on our behalf. Bless the offering they bring—themselves. May they find your promised blessing, both in what they have freely given and in what they have given up.

Comfort families, for the deployment is also theirs. Their sacrifices are every bit as costly. You promise comfort to those who mourn. Our souls cry out against loss because it was never meant to be so. But you, oh God, have brought us redemption through loss. Do it again daily for our soldiers and their families. Bind up the brokenhearted. Pour into them the *oil of gladness*. Transform their despair into songs of praise. Do it for our nation as we grieve the losses of the past seven years.

In Jesus' name, Amen.

VALUED

"Can a mother forget the baby at her breast and have no compassion on the child she has borne? Though she may forget, I will not forget you! See, I have engraved you on the palms of my hands; your walls are ever before me."
—Isaiah 49:15-16

America has not always valued her sons and daughters who have returned from wars and conflicts. At times, we have laid upon their shoulders the burden of accountability for an unpopular war, and we have questioned the motives of those who have gone in obedience to serve their country. Greater than the wounds of combat are those inflicted when a soldier feels forgotten by the very people for whom the sacrifices are made.

I pray for our soldiers and for us. May every decision to engage in military involvement come from a posture of prayer, humility, and necessity.

I also pray that the popularity of any particular conflict will never be the scale upon which we weigh the value of a soldier's service. Deployment is and has always been costly for both soldiers and families. Wherever we come down on the side of war, I pray that we may recognize and value each soldier's sacrifice.

May the safety and support of American sons and daughters in harm's way be paramount in governmental decisions. In soldiers' moments of deepest loneliness, weariness, deprivation, and danger, I want them to feel with certainty that they are *engraved on the palms of your hands*, Lord, and lifted up in our thoughts and prayers. I want them to know that our eyes are ever looking eagerly for their return. May our words and deeds communicate our gratitude for sacrifices made.

Is the calling of a soldier less valuable than the calling of a peacemaker in a world where evil is real? Perhaps this is something we are not equipped to judge. Instead, I pray that we will devote ourselves to pray and work for peace and then trust that the hand of Providence is working—even in the soldier's camp.

In Jesus' name, Amen.

SEPTEMBER 21, 2008

ENDURANCE

. . . And let us run with endurance the race that is set before us, looking unto Jesus, the author and finisher of our faith, who for the joy that was set before Him endured the cross. . . . Consider him . . . lest you become weary and discouraged in your souls.

—Hebrews 12:1-3 NKJV

War stretches the human capacity like almost no other earthly experience can. Only those who have lived it are qualified to testify to it. I am *not* qualified, but because I love a soldier who is now deployed, I am drawn to stories from the front, trying to find some point of reference from which to pray. I come up dreadfully short of any real understanding, but still I am compelled to pray, even in general terms.

I pray for physical endurance, Lord. Grant soldiers restorative sleep whenever they can seize the opportunity to rest. Blot out the sounds, aches, pains, fears, and stresses that might rob them of sleep. Grant them health and bring swift healing when illness and injury occur. When one is weak, bring them someone who can share their strength. Guard hearts and minds from the strain of prolonged stress and hardship. Shield them from crushing loneliness. Grant them frequent opportunities for contact with loved ones. Remind us to be faithful in our encouragement and remembrances. Grant them the ability to endure deadening routines from which there is no escape. Provide creative outlets for recreation and renewal. Guide chaplains to mine from your Word its treasures and comforts.

Help soldiers to think of Christ as the perfect model of endurance and find hope in his example.

It has been said that out of the presses of pain come the soul's best wine. Will you bless the adversities and sufferings of our soldiers and bring from them a rare and valued wine? And do not forget the winepresses here at home that are tread by the soldiers' families.

In Jesus' name, Amen.

LEADERSHIP

Blessed is the nation whose God is the LORD.
—Psalm 33:12

Pray for kings and others in power, so that we may live quiet
and peaceful lives as we worship and honor God.
—1 Timothy 2:2 CEV

There is great power in leadership. Leaders can inspire
acts of great courage and noble sacrifice. They can also sway
the masses to unthinkable acts of violence and atrocity. How
important, then, is the command to pray for our leaders?

As we prepare to choose the leadership for our nation, we
seek your guidance, Lord. Give us wisdom and discernment.
We see only the public image, but you see the heart. Guide us
to leaders who are practical enough to realize they do not have
all the answers and humble enough to accept their dependence
on you and others. We pray for leaders whose chief aim is the
smile of God's approval and good done for humankind. We
pray for leaders committed to the safety and support of our
men and women deployed around the globe.

Raise up responsible and discerning military leaders at every
level—servant leaders who lead by honorable example, model
integrity, and hate war. We pray for leaders who are strong in
the might of humility and not arrogant. Summon leaders who
will stand strong in the face of criticism, guided by principle
and unmoved by changing political winds. Call leaders who
are builders of unity and ambassadors of reconciliation. Make

us more faithful to support our leaders, both civilian and military, with our prayers, and less ready to level them with our criticism.

Thank you for the men and women willing to shoulder the awesome responsibility of leadership. Bless them and equip them with extraordinary wisdom and a sincere love for those they serve.

In Jesus' name, Amen.

DETOUR

But I trust in you, O LORD; I say, "You are my God." My times are in your hands.

—Psalm 31:14-15

Be very careful, then, how you live—not as unwise but as wise, making the most of every opportunity, because the days are evil.

—Ephesians 5:15-16

When you pass through the waters, I will be with you; and when you pass through the rivers, they will not sweep over you. When you walk through the fire, you will not be burned; the flames will not set you ablaze.

—Isaiah 43:2

I left for work at the usual time, expecting my commute to be like every other. And then I saw the *Detour* sign. Road construction forced everyone onto a series of twisted country roads, inching along at a snail's pace. I had not planned for this. Frustration consumed me. Life's journey includes detours that interrupt, change plans, get us lost, and test our limits.

I pray for deployed soldiers and their families who may be finding their *detour* much harder and longer than they ever expected. When they can neither retreat nor advance, I pray that you will come to their sides and walk them through it. Coach them in the difficult lessons of faith, trust, and patience. Give them direction when they feel utterly lost. Keep them safe along the way. Help them to relinquish their struggle with the situation and trust you with the destination.

When doubt and discouragement settle in and dominate their thoughts—when they feel angry at you, God, because life is hard and you seem so unfair, help them understand that life and God are not the same. There are no immunity clauses in life, but you have promised that you will go through life's storms with us. Your love will prevail when we put our trust in you. Perhaps the hardest part is the tyranny of time. It cannot be sped up. You just have to inch through it. Help soldiers and families entrust those tedious, dragging, exasperating moments into your redeeming hands. Open their eyes to see every moment of life as a reason for gratitude. Bless their detour. May it refine their perspective, character, and values to make the rest of life richer.

In Jesus' name, Amen.

FAITHFULNESS

His master replied, "Well done, good and faithful servant! You have been faithful with a few things; I will put you in charge of many things. Come and share your master's happiness!"

—Matthew 25:21

But the fruit of the Spirit is love, joy, peace, patience, kindness, goodness, faithfulness, gentleness and self-control.

—Galatians 5:22-23

In our present world view, we have rewritten Jesus' parable of the talents to place the emphasis on success. We might even rephrase his words: "Well done, rich and successful servant! Good return on your money!" While diligence surely played a role in growing the talents these men had been given, it was the character trait of faithfulness that Jesus commended. We focus on success or failure, but those are God's concerns, not ours. His eyes are on our faithfulness.

I pray for our troops and their families to grasp hold of this truth and let it be the compass that keeps them on course. Close their ears to the countless voices who may judge their mission a success or failure, and help them focus on faithfully doing their day-to-day jobs. Wise was the person who said it is easier for an athlete to win an Olympic contest than it is to rise up every morning and keep on keeping on, when plans may not come to fulfillment, desired results are painfully slow in coming, obstacles arise at every turn, and when hopes are dashed and sorrows mount. It is *who* we are that matters. Can we still bless God? Can we still help others? Can we still press on?

I pray for soldiers and families to have a tenacious constancy in the face of discouragement, to remain dedicated when it runs counter to everything they see and feel. Drawing on your strength and grace, Lord, help them fulfill the daily tasks set before them, striving for the only goal worth life or death: to hear you say, "Well done, good and faithful servant!" Produce in them the fruit of faithfulness, and may they share the Master's happiness.

In Jesus' name, Amen.

PERSPECTIVE

Trust in the LORD with all your heart and lean not on your own understanding; in all your ways acknowledge him, and he will make your paths straight.

—Proverbs 3:5-6

"For my thoughts are not your thoughts, neither are your ways my ways," declares the LORD.

—Isaiah 55:8

I have always thought that children's literature contained some pretty profound truths for the discerning eye. *Look Book* by Tana Hoban is one of those books. It is a simple picture book, in which each page is like a camera lens zoomed into a tiny portion of a larger picture. Given the small frame of magnified detail, you, the reader, get to guess what the larger picture is before you turn the page and confirm your interpretation. Is that not like life? In life, we only see a tiny portion of the big picture. It always feels magnified, and we react to our interpretation of the details, whether we are right or wrong. Sometimes the details are so dark and obscure that we could never imagine they are part of a larger picture, one that is actually quite beautiful, with the darks providing the contrast that draws out its beauty.

I pray for soldiers and families staring into a small circle of life that contains neither a hint of beauty nor a single detail that makes any sense. Father, this is a time when they must let go of trying to look for the goodness and meaning in such tangled details and trust you with the big picture. We are trying to see in time what you see in eternity, but our lens does not have a wide enough angle. This is a time to put down the picture and study the artist instead. Turn their focus toward the changeless character of the one who demonstrated his love and goodness by wrapping himself in human flesh, coming to experience everything we must experience, living the sinless life we failed to live, and dying in our place to satisfy the demands of justice against our sin. We can trust a love that deep with the details of the big picture. Work the dark contrasts of this difficult life experience into a work of beauty that will take their breath away.

In Jesus' name, Amen.

GRACE

"And besides all this, between us and you a great chasm has been fixed, so that those who want to go from here to you cannot, nor can anyone cross over from there to us."
—Luke 16:26

Love is very patient and kind. . . .Love does not demand its own way. It is not irritable or touchy. . . .If you love someone you will be loyal to him no matter what the cost. You will always believe in him, always expect the best of him, and always stand your ground in defending him.
—1 Corinthians 13:4, 5, 7 The Living Bible

I know that the great chasm referred to in the sixteenth chapter of Luke is the chasm between heaven and hell that no man can breach, but in some ways it also hints at a reality that soldiers on deployment and their families face. Where families once shared daily life experiences that bound them together in a common history and understanding, the soldier's new realm of experiences cannot be fully shared and understood by loved ones. For this piece of a soldier's life, comrades are often closer than family. At the same time, families going on with day-to-day life are being shaped by experiences and crises the soldier does not share. In some sense, a chasm is put between them. Every soldier brings back a story. For some, it remains locked inside, because no words can adequately tell it.

Father, it is especially for these soldiers that I pray. This is a gulf that only grace can bridge. May love and grace span the gulf where words and understanding fail. May soldiers and families feel the liberty to bring their unspoken burdens to the one who called himself the Great Burden Bearer. I pray for sensitivity and realistic expectations among both soldiers and families as they confront the chasms that formed without their consent. Weed out of their lives any roots of resentment, guilt, or indifference. Pour into them your own love and grace as they rebuild their bridges. Give them a persevering heart until the perfect bond of unity is restored.

In the name of the one whose sacrificial love bridges the great chasm separating man from God, Amen.

WISDOM

But where is wisdom found? No human knows the way. . . .
God is the only one who knows the way to wisdom, because
he sees everything beneath the heavens.
—Job 28:12-13, 23-24 CEV

If any of you need wisdom, you should ask God, and it will
be given to you. God is generous and won't correct you for
asking. But when you ask for something, you must have
faith and not doubt.
—James 1:5-6 CEV

A soldier's eye is on the hand of his commander. At his
signal, the soldier moves. Trust is implicit, for in the moment
of decisive action a soldier responds with a faith and obedience that was previously decided. Otherwise, who could stand
in battle? How critical it is, then, to have a commander who
is exemplary in character and leadership, guided by wisdom,
humbled by the weight of responsibility he carries, and ever
mindful of the sacredness of the lives entrusted to his care.

Eternal, all-wise God, as we stand on the eve of choosing
the next Commander in Chief, whose decisions will impact all
who serve under him and live under his authority, we ask you
for wisdom. Give us the ability to discern the inner qualities
and judgment worthy of the trust of soldier and civilian alike.

Since *God is the only one who knows the way to wisdom
because he sees everything beneath the heavens,* we come on
behalf of our soldiers, who will pledge their obedience to their

41

commanders' orders. We come on behalf of our nation, whose very foundations are being shaken. We take a stand on our knees today, Lord. Counsel us (Ps. 16:7). Bring understanding and light to the minds of ordinary people (Ps. 119:130). Raise up the leader worthy of our trust—the one upon whose heart you have laid the burden of love for this nation.

Thank you for inviting us to come to you for wisdom. Now grant us the faith to believe you have heard our prayer and will answer.

In the name of Jesus, Amen.

REST AND RENEWAL

"Six days you shall labor, but on the seventh day you shall rest; even during the plowing season and harvest you must rest."

—Exodus 34:21

He [Jesus] withdrew by boat privately to a solitary place.

—Matthew 14:13

A cheerful heart is good medicine.

—Proverbs 17:22

"Come to me, all you who are weary and burdened, and I will give you rest."

—Matthew 11:28

Life is often very heavy. Responsibilities, disappointments, fears, illness, losses, stress, and fatigue press in on our bodies and minds until we feel like we will crack. We feel our frailty and lack of power and are desperate for relief. God understands. Jesus often withdrew to a solitary place to find renewal. We were created with body, soul, and spirit, and God planned for the care of all three because they are so interconnected. He gave us the Sabbath principle. It is visible in nature with seasons of dormancy and rest.

Father, who more than soldiers have tested the extremes of life's harshness? Long days with little rest or sleep melt into weeks, and even months, until *fatigue* becomes an inadequate word to describe their physical state. Bodies break down under stress. How can one even imagine the stress of such an environment of loneliness, uncertainty, deprivation, fear, and death, or the sadness that deployment brings? From such an environment you cannot just walk away. And what about the spirit? What could challenge faith and hope more than the dark questions of war?

Our prayer today is for our soldiers' rest and the renewal of their bodies, souls, and spirits. We ask for restorative sleep that renews the body and for a time that blots out the awareness of pressures that weigh so heavily on the mind. We ask for Sabbath moments in the midst of wearying days—times when a sweet memory, a scene in nature, an unexpected treat from home, a comrade's encouragement, or some divine encounter will lift the burden for a time. We pray for creative, spontaneous, and recreational moments that will help release the stress. Grant them the gift of healing laughter. We bring them to you in prayer, the weary and burdened, and ask on their behalf that you would fulfill your promise to give them rest. Enable them to feel the peaceful comfort and safety of your strong and loving arms and rest there as little children for a time.

In Jesus' name, Amen.

FREEDOM

It is for freedom that Christ has set us free. Stand firm, then, and do not let yourselves be burdened again by a yoke of slavery.

—Galatians 5:1

"Freely you have received, freely give."

—Matthew 10:8

Freedom is defined as the absence of coercion or constraint in choice or action and the liberation from restraint or power of another. As a people who have enjoyed great freedom, I wonder how we view it. Do we consider it a right, entitlement, or privilege, or do we see it as a costly gift that is purchased at a great price?

This past week we celebrated Veterans' Day, a day set aside to honor and remember those in the past and present who have defended our nation. Was it just another day off? Did we think about the truth that our freedom has cost someone dearly? Do we understand that someone gave up their freedom, at least for a time, to secure our own? The principle of the Cross is still being lived out in our world today.

Every soldier and every soldier's family has given up something of their own freedom so that others' freedom will be secured. We have previously considered some of the costs that soldiers and families bear: unrepeatable moments with family, comfort, safety, health, and even life itself. So why do they do it? For pay? Hardly! For bravado? Perhaps for some. But the only motive powerful enough to sustain them when fear, death, loneliness, and darkness of soul closes in on them is love—love of the liberty to live free of the coercion and control of another and pursue happiness for themselves and those they love. The human soul cries out for freedom because free will is a gift from God. God understood that love cannot exist in an atmosphere of coercion.

Lord, bless all who have given up their freedom and those who continue to do so that we still might enjoy it. They have followed your example. As they have freely given, so may they and their families freely receive your blessings and rewards. Give us all a heart of gratitude for the sacrifices that have purchased our freedom.

In Jesus' name, Amen.

CARRIED

There you saw how the LORD your God carried you, as a father carries his son, all the way you went until you reached this place.

—Deuteronomy 1:31

The calendar holds a unique power of influence in our lives. It takes an ordinary day, like every other day, and infuses it with meaning and remembrances that can draw us through the whole spectrum of emotion—from unshakeable sorrow and regret to unspeakable joy and thanksgiving. It is the vehicle we use to intentionally recall important events so that we do not forget the foundational experiences that have shaped our lives—the memories we need to keep us on course. Calendar dates mark our celebrations and traditions. They are often days when routine schedules are set aside and people take precedence over duties. Aren't most special calendar events centered on people, such as birthdays, deaths, anniversaries, remembrances of people who have had a unique influence in our history, and sacrificial actions taken by people we honor by remembrance? Expectations and longings run high, but life so often disappoints. I find my own heart drifting toward the sad end of the spectrum as I think of the upcoming holiday season, knowing my soldier son will be missing that precious family time that every heart longs for.

I pray for my son and the countless thousands of soldiers and families who will face the challenge of disappointed expectations and unfulfilled longings during this holiday season. I pray the message of the familiar poem, *Footprints in the Sand*—that you will carry them through this difficult time as a father carries his son. May your presence be somehow tangible to them and uplift them. Provide moments of contact with loved ones. Surprise them with unexpected joys. May the very things they miss the most validate the importance of what they are serving to protect. May the bonds between comrades ease their loneliness. As stars seem to shine brighter in the darkest night, let the value of home and relationships be heightened by a deepening sense of gratitude so that the day of homecoming will be even sweeter.

Father, we give thanks for the soldiers who serve and the families who serve with them. Bless them with joys that transcend their circumstances—the joys you promise in giving.

In Jesus' name, Amen.

UNFINISHED BUSINESS

As a mother comforts her child, so will I comfort you.
—Isaiah 66:13

Praise be to the God and Father of our Lord Jesus Christ, the Father of compassion and the God of all comfort, who comforts us in all our troubles.
—2 Corinthians 1:3-4

"I am the Alpha and the Omega," says the Lord God, "who is, and who was, and who is to come, the Almighty."
—Revelation 1:8

We mostly go through life engaged in the consuming busy-ness of work, family, and social obligations and are essentially unaware of the unique heartaches people all around us are experiencing. Then something happens and our eyes are opened. Perhaps we have hit our own crisis, and now we understand the sorrows and struggles of others because it has become personal. This week, as a family member's death became an imminent possibility, for the first time I thought about what it would be like for a soldier on deployment to receive word of a loss back home. What is it like to know the regret of not having the chance to say goodbye to loved ones, extended family, or friends who die while a soldier is on the other side of the world? There is no opportunity for the soldier to pay respects or share in fellowship with family in times of grief, telling the bittersweet stories of remembrance that are such an important part of letting go. The grief process is thwarted, and burdens pile up on an already heavy heart.

Father, I pray for soldiers who are prevented by deployments from finding closure in times of loss. Walk with them through their solitary grief. Carry this extraordinary burden for them. Bring them comrades who will listen to their stories. Comfort families who miss that critical support of a deployed loved one at such vulnerable times. Provide an outlet for expression of grief so it does not get bottled up inside. Great God, who is unbound by the confines of time and capable of redeeming the past that is beyond our influence, walk with soldiers through the unfinished business of coming to peace with the unattended deaths that are now in their past.

In Jesus' name, Amen.

A LIVING GIFT

"For God so loved the world that he gave his one and only Son, that whoever believes in him shall not perish but have eternal life. For God did not send his Son into the world to condemn the world, but to save the world through him."
—John 3:16-17

This is how we know what love is: Jesus Christ laid down his life for us. And we ought to lay down our lives for our brothers.
—1 John 3:16

At its foundation, the Christmas story illustrates the essence of giving—the giving of a son who would live the sinless life we fail to live and die a substitutionary death that would fully satisfy the justice of a holy God against our sin. Even the hardest and most unbelieving among us gets drawn into the spirit of giving when Christmas comes around. We want to express love and gratitude through the gifts we give, but the motive and intent so often gets corrupted by our busy materialistic culture. We so easily get caught in a reciprocal short circuit. In other words, we *have* to give because someone gave to *us*.

An old movie offers a timely message. *Pay It Forward* is the poignant story of a young boy who took to heart a social studies assignment to think of something one person could do to change the world. His idea: instead of *paying back* a favor, *pay it forward* with an act of kindness to three new people. What initially seemed like a disappointing failure became like a pebble dropped into a pond, rippling out to its very edges. Essentially, the rules of paying it forward were that the payer must somehow help three people, perhaps by doing something for them that they cannot do themselves, and in exchange, the recipients must promise to pay it forward to three others.

Father, I think first of the gift you gave us. You did for us what we could not do for ourselves, and I pray that in gratitude we will pay it forward. I especially think of our soldiers deployed around the world and the sacrifice shared by their families. I wonder: do they realize that they are paying it forward? Wherever they are needed, they willingly go to help people who cannot help themselves. They endure great stress, deprivation, loneliness, and danger to give a hand to desperate people. I pray that you will not only protect them but bless the living gifts they give. May it so touch the lives of even the most suspicious and ungrateful recipients that their hearts may be changed. Especially open the eyes of children and youth to a hope that is much greater than retribution and revenge. May they feel challenged to pay the gift forward to others around them and so change the world, one life at a time. Generous God, multiply the impact of the living gifts soldiers and their families are giving around the world this Christmas.

In Jesus' name, Amen.

VISITATION

And the Word became flesh and dwelt among us.

—John 1:14 NKJV

There is something about a visit from the Commander in Chief in times of war that infuses the troops with renewed hope, loyalty, and perseverance. He has put himself at risk and pushed aside every other duty to come to his soldiers as one of them, and say, "You matter to me. I understand the depth of your sacrifice."

All of us have the need to be understood, to have someone validate our thoughts, feelings, and needs. I have watched the tears of frustration of the stroke victim or the autistic child who struggles to communicate a need or thought, but no one understands. Eventually, the soul grows silent and gives up. At every stage of life and in every circumstance, we search for someone who understands what we are going through. Teens stick together like glue. New parents organize play dates. People grappling with the pain of illness or loss join support groups. Soldiers form life-long allegiances with veteran groups. Nothing is more isolating or soul crushing than having no one who understands.

The good news of Christmas is that the Eternal God clothed himself in human flesh and visited earth—not only to be the sinless substitute whose sacrificial death would satisfy the wrath of God against our sin, but also so that he would perfectly understand us. He understands the human existence because he lived it with us. Whatever we face, he has been there before us and has overcome it so that he can help us in every circumstance.

I pray that this will be good news for soldiers who are far from home this Christmas. Walk with them in the military camps, mess halls, and front lines. Affirm their thoughts and feelings—their loneliness, fears, fatigue, sagging morale, and questions, as one who understands. Discern their heart needs and graciously meet them. As Commander in Chief, encourage them to faithfully press on toward the finish line and not give up. Give them the eyes to see that God is in their midst. Keep them safe and healthy. Lead them to experience the real blessing of Christmas, apart from the superficial trappings that so easily distract us here at home.

In Jesus' name, Amen.

REMEMBERING

The LORD said to Moses, "Speak to the Israelites and say to them: 'These are my appointed feasts, the appointed feasts of the LORD, which you are to proclaim as sacred assemblies.'"

—Leviticus 23:1-2

And he took bread, gave thanks and broke it, and gave it to them, saying, "This is my body given for you; do this in remembrance of me."

—Luke 22:19

As we come to the close of another year, much focus will be given to the events of 2008. News media will dissect, analyze, and judge decisions, leaders, administrations, and wars. Looking back serves an important function if we are wise enough to look for the lessons and guiding principles rather than blame and judge. God puts high priority on remembering.

The Hebrew calendar year was outlined with festivals and sacred assemblies of remembrance that the people were commanded to celebrate. Jesus also commanded us to partake of Communion *in remembrance* of him. The tangible, visible expressions of all these celebrations were intended to draw the attention of the people of God to himself—his love, faithfulness, deliverance, protection, provision, guidance, forgiveness, and fellowship.

Father, as this year comes to a close—a year of wars, deployments, separations, sacrifice, and extraordinary stresses—draw our attention to your great faithfulness. Help us see the lessons and guiding principles that the unique circumstances of 2008 can teach us about you and about us. We remember your protection with thanksgiving, as we have been spared any attacks on our homeland. We remember all the days you have preserved our soldiers' lives. For those who laid down life itself, we remember their sacrifice and we remember your self-proclamation as the God of all comfort. Console those hurting families.

We give thanks for your faithful provision—for the physical sustenance, grace, strength, and endurance you have provided soldiers and families during the extraordinary stresses of deployment. We remember your mercy in our human failures. In the midst of trial and evil, you have still worked for our good, refining us in ways that ease and plenty can never do. We remember and take comfort in your sovereignty over all things and pray for the fulfillment of your good purposes and plans. As we step into a new year, we do so with our hand in yours. Continue your protection, provision, and blessing upon our soldiers and their families. Bring to remembrance the lessons of your faithfulness that soldiers, families, and we as a nation might find our hope and confidence in you.

In Jesus' name, Amen.

SERVING

Your attitude should be the same as that of Christ Jesus: Who, being in very nature God, did not consider equality with God something to be grasped, but made himself nothing, taking the very nature of a servant, being made in human likeness.

—Philippians 2:5-7

Do not be overawed when a man grows rich, when the splendor of his house increases; for he will take nothing with him when he dies, his splendor will not descend with him.

—Psalm 49:16-17

Something about the start of a new year pushes us to take stock of where we are and where we want to be. Resolutions are crafted as we try to hold ourselves accountable to a higher standard than we have achieved. Perhaps we realize how quickly time passes and decide there are some things we want to be more intentional about while we still have the chance.

I once read a question that someone used to begin their self-assessment: who do you most admire and why? If you are an American and have a TV in your house, you would probably at least be tempted to list some sports figure, actor, singer, artist, successful businessman, or influential leader. We have been led to equate greatness with success, talent, power, and recognition. Would we include on our list a single mom or dad who has faithfully served their family, the person who volunteers at the soup kitchen or homeless shelter, the guy who shovels snow for the elderly couple down the street, or the soldier serving somewhere around the globe?

Father, realign our understanding of greatness in light of your Son, who laid aside glory to serve. Help us to see that true greatness comes in the form of humble service. I lift up soldiers all around the world who are enduring harsh conditions, extreme pressures, lonely separations, and perilous circumstances as they faithfully serve their country. They will not become famous. They will not accumulate wealth. They will not be applauded or even understood. Still, they go and serve where they are called to serve. Bless them for their sacrificial service. May their rewards be greater than those measured by dollars and cents. Reward them with wisdom, character, and gratitude. I lift up families who serve by permission, accepting hardship, loneliness, exceptional stress, and sometimes financial need and obscurity, as they stick faithfully by their soldier loved ones. Grant them rewards of the heart.

I pray for soldiers' children to see serving as a worthy model to emulate wherever life may take them. Give us all a discerning eye to recognize the greatness of serving and give honor where honor is due. Help us set our hearts on what is of lasting value and of admirable character, as we contemplate who we are and who we want to be.

In honor of our great example, Jesus, Amen.

JANUARY 11, 2009

ANCHORED

This hope is like a firm and steady anchor for our souls. In fact, hope reaches behind the curtain and into the most holy place. Jesus has gone there ahead of us.

—Hebrews 6:19-20 CEV

When darkness veils His lovely face, I rest on His unchanging grace; In every high and stormy gale, my anchor holds within the vale.

—From Edward Mote's hymn, "The Solid Rock"

It is amazing how much the human mind and body can endure. I have personally witnessed courageous battles against cancer and debilitating diseases, people rising to face another day of depression or incalculable loss, and smiles on the faces of children who will live life strapped in a wheel chair. Examples of resilience and endurance are innumerable. Yet we have all known frailty. We have been worn down, sad, empty, and we have lost our grip on hope. From a feeling perspective, we are all done! Surely, many soldiers on long deployments under extraordinary pressures have been there, too. They are pressed beyond exhaustion. Bodies begin to break down under stress. Minds have recorded unspeakable things that cannot be erased. In the very least, they have encountered troubling, unanswerable questions. Hearts have known loneliness that nothing eases. How critical to have an anchor when you are way beyond your own ability to hold fast.

Years ago, I encountered a verse that profoundly impacted me:

Three men were walking on a wall,
Feeling, Faith, and Fact,
When Feeling got an awful fall,
And Faith was taken back.
So close was Faith to Feeling,
He stumbled and fell too,
But Fact remained,
And pulled Faith back,
And Faith brought Feeling too.[5]

How true that our stability and security fall first in the area of feelings. When we are tired and vulnerable, we fall off the wall of hope, trust, and will. Because faith is so closely tied to our feelings, faith is often pulled down, too. It is only fact that remains as an anchor, able to pull back faith and, in time, feeling.

Father, as I think of deployed soldiers and their families, I pray that you anchor them in truth. They are loved, and their service is not empty or unnoticed. You are sovereign, and you can take what is evil and painful and bring good from it. Your presence is always with them, your mercy stands eager to forgive every repentant heart, your love embraces all people, and you are able to protect, provide, sustain, and keep them secure. For those who have slipped off the wall temporarily, pull them back. Help them get a grip on truths that will anchor them. Heal the wounds that have happened in the fall.

In Jesus' name, Amen.

COURAGE

When they saw the courage of Peter and John and realized that they were unschooled, ordinary men, they were astonished and they took note that these men had been with Jesus.

—Acts 4:13

"But now I urge you to keep up your courage, because not one of you will be lost; only the ship will be destroyed. Last night an angel of the God whose I am and whom I serve stood beside me and said, '. . . God has graciously given you the lives of all who sail with you.' . . . Nevertheless, we must run aground on some island."

—Acts 27:22-23, 24, 26

My flesh and my heart may fail, but God is the strength of my heart and my portion forever.

—Psalm 73:26

Be strong and of good courage is a common lesson of Scripture. Courage, simply defined, is mental or moral strength. It is more than just the willingness to face danger—though putting oneself in harm's way for the benefit of others certainly counts as courageous. Continuing to press on in difficult circumstances and standing for what you value in the face of great criticism and consequences also fit the definition of courage. Courage, then, is not only the realm of the elite warrior, but of ordinary men and women, as emphasized by the passage above.

As I pray for soldiers to be men and women of courage, I think not only of the valiant who face grave risk on behalf of others but also of those who continue to press on under extraordinary physical, mental, and moral pressures. I lift up families whose mental and moral strength is equally challenged. For every soldier and family member I pray the hope of Psalm 73:26—that when in human weakness they may falter, God would be the strength of their heart and portion. Father, take these ordinary men and women and make them great in your strength. Then let their example give hope and courage to others whose steps are faltering.

As surely as the sun will rise tomorrow, life will always have that *nevertheless* clause. In the above story from the twenty-seventh chapter of Acts, Paul was promised by an angel of God that everyone on the ship on which he was sailing would be saved, but *nevertheless* the ship would indeed run aground. The terror of that event would have to be faced. Lord, Give every soldier and family member the mental and moral strength to face their *nevertheless* experience.

In the name of Jesus, our courageous example, Amen.

NEED

Listen to my cry, for I am in desperate need.

—Psalm 142:6

For he will deliver the needy who cry out, the afflicted who have no one to help.

—Psalm 72:12

. . . Whoever is kind to the needy honors God.

—Proverbs 14:31

If anyone has material possessions and sees his brother in need but has no pity on him, how can the love of God be in him?

—1 John 3:17

As a proud and prosperous nation, we have been raised to believe we can have whatever we want if we try hard enough. We expect it to be so. Still, we find ourselves in a place where the foundations of prosperity are being seriously shaken. We may be forced to make a more honest distinction between wants and needs. Each of us personally knows someone who has been laid off in the past few months. I think about the impact on military families. A soldier's wage is hardly adequate to begin with. Most soldiers depend on supplemental income from spouses or family members. What will they do when their pink slips come? When deployed soldiers return, will the companies they worked for still exist? Will those companies be able to offer the same level of position to the soldier who left to serve? What about wounded and disabled soldiers who find it hard to compete for a job when the employment rate is good? Who will help veterans who are completely dependent on VA benefits and charitable organizations when funds dry up?

Father, the message of Scripture is clear—you care deeply for those in need, and we honor you when we help the needy. I pray for military families who may be experiencing unprecedented need. I pray that they would cry out to you in their need. Mobilize us to meet those needs as you bring them to our awareness. Preserve the jobs of soldiers returning from deployment so that they will not be exchanging one set of extreme pressures for another and lose hope. Provide for the needs of wounded and disabled soldiers who have given freely of themselves and come home broken. Help us as a nation redefine greatness, so that it is less about prosperity, privilege, and power, and more about how we care for every one of our citizens—especially those in need. Give us today our daily bread, and a willing heart to share it with those in need.

In Jesus' name, Amen.

TESTED

But he knows the way that I take; when he has tested me, I will come forth as gold.

—Job 23:10

Blessed is the man who perseveres under trial, because when he has stood the test, he will receive the crown of life that God has promised to those who love him.

—James 1:12

"Take out your test booklet and your pencils. You may begin."

Those were the familiar test instructions heard so often throughout our years of formal education. You hoped you would be prepared, but there was always anxious concern that something would be asked of you that would catch you off guard. Sooner or later, life is that professor who throws something at you for which you were not prepared. Soldiers and families encounter it all the time. So much training and disciplined preparation is invested into maintaining a state of readiness for the test, but no one gets the questions ahead of time. If only it could be a test of what you know. Instead, it is mostly about who you are inside—the internal reserve you have to draw on when every earthly prop has been knocked out from under you.

Father, I pray for soldiers on deployment who are being tested beyond anything they could ever have imagined. Call forth from their reserves the strength they did not think they had. Remind them that your reserves are limitless and available to anyone who asks for them. Guard their minds so they are not crushed by the extraordinary pressures they must bear. Give them the peace that transcends human understanding—the peace that comes from knowing that you are in control, and the outcome is in your hands. Pour your strength into them when they have nothing left to give. Strengthen the bond of brotherhood among soldiers so that they are committed to helping each other make it through. Rein in every anxious and despairing thought and help them focus on the task at hand. Enable them to see, in their mind's eye, the finish line, and your sovereign, loving hands bringing them across it. Be merciful to soldiers who do not do well on the test and help them be merciful to themselves. Give them eyes to see your loving hand reaching down to lift them back up. Thank you that it is not the passing or failing grade that matters, but the refining to an ore of greater purity, strength, and value through your grace. Bless this time of testing to that end.

In the name of the one who faced the supreme test of all, our Savior, Amen.

PEACE

"Peace I leave with you; my peace I give you. I do not give to you as the world gives. Do not let your hearts be troubled and do not be afraid."

—John 14:27

And the peace of God, which transcends all understanding, will guard your hearts and your minds in Christ Jesus.

—Philippians 4:7

A furious squall came up, and the waves broke over the boat, so that it was nearly swamped. Jesus was in the stern, sleeping on a cushion. The disciples woke him and said to him, "Teacher, don't you care if we drown?" He got up, rebuked the wind and said to the waves, "Quiet! Be still!" Then the wind died down and it was completely calm.

—Mark 4:37-39

If you were given a blank canvas, a set of paints, and the assignment to paint a picture entitled "Peace," what would it look like? A golden, serene landscape? A quiet pool? A sleeping infant? A cemetery? Would the details reflect idyllic circumstances? I would not imagine that any of us would paint a lightning pierced tempest like the one in the story above. Our inclination is to see peace as intricately connected to the right set of circumstances. The great power of Christ's words ("Peace, be still") would never have been witnessed if the disciples had not been in a storm great enough to threaten death. Without that experience, they would never have known how safe they really were in his hands. Peace is one of those paradoxes in life. The deepest, most enduring peace is often discovered in the midst of the greatest conflict.

Father, as you have done with trees that have endured great storms, send down the deepest roots on our windward side. We grow more secure by the very storms that threaten our peace. It is that kind of peace I pray that our deployed soldiers would know—peace that is rooted in something deeper than circumstances, peace that transcends logic. The disciples lost their peace when they focused on the storm and lost sight of who was in the boat with them. I pray that soldiers and their families would have a profound sense that they are not in the boat alone. The one who speaks and the wind obeys is there with them. Whatever tempests may arise, may they only force deeper root systems that will enable soldiers to stand strong and secure. Father, so many of the soldiers are tender, young trees who have not experienced enough of life to have deep, securing roots. Plant them between soldiers who have grown deep roots—men and women who can brace them in the storms. Help us all get past our dread of the tempests and dare to discover the peace that transcends understanding hidden within.

In the name of the Prince of Peace, Amen.

> The wind that blows can never kill
> The tree God plants;
> It bloweth east, it bloweth west,
> The tender leaves have little rest,
> But any wind that blows is best.
> The tree that God plants
> Strikes deeper root, grows higher still,
> Spreads greater boughs, for God's good will
> Meets all its wants.[6]

TEMPTED

No temptation has seized you except what is common to man. And God is faithful; he will not let you be tempted beyond what you can bear. But when you are tempted, he will also provide a way out so that you can stand up under it.

—1 Corinthians 10:13

. . . And we take captive every thought to make it obedient to Christ.

—2 Corinthians 10:5

The tempter came to him and said, "If you are the Son of God, tell these stones to become bread." Jesus answered, "It is written: 'Man does not live on bread alone, but on every word that comes from the mouth of God.'"

—Matthew 4:3-4

As much as I would like to think of myself as a reasonably strong person, certain things make me especially vulnerable to wrong choices. Fatigue is certainly one of them. Everything looks clouded through weary eyes. Pain is another. There are times when I would do almost anything to find temporary relief, even if it would mean a costly gamble in the long run. Loneliness is a powerful black hole.

Pride, pleasure, control, fear, and deception—the snares are many. None of us can avoid encounters with temptation. Even Jesus had his wilderness challenge. I pray for soldiers and families, upon whom so many of these stumbling blocks converge all at once—fatigue, loss, loneliness, fear, and unrelenting stress. Deliver them from costly choices made in moments of great vulnerability. Help them recognize the dangers and choose the way of escape that you have promised. May you be the strong tower they run to for safety when temptation closes in. Christ's victory over temptation came in knowing and trusting the Word of God.

Lord, help soldiers and families see that there is a correlation between preparedness and victory that extends beyond the literal battlefield. It is just as critical to be prepared for the battlefields of the heart and mind. It is there that renegade thoughts must be taken captive. Let the knowledge of what *is written* give them ready response in moments of temptation. Remind them that there is no guilt in experiencing temptation—only in succumbing to it. May those familiar words from your ancient prayer come immediately to their lips: "Lead us away from temptation and deliver us from evil."

In Jesus' name, Amen.

HOPE

Yet this I call to mind and therefore I have hope: Because of the LORD's great love we are not consumed, for his compassions never fail. They are new every morning; great is your faithfulness.

—Lamentations 3:21-23

But those who hope in the LORD will renew their strength. They will soar on wings like eagles; they will run and not grow weary, they will walk and not be faint.

—Isaiah 40:31

We have this hope as an anchor for the soul, firm and secure. It enters the inner sanctuary behind the curtain, where Jesus, who went before us, has entered on our behalf. He has become a high priest forever.

—Hebrews 6:19-20

Not only so, but we also rejoice in our sufferings, because we know that suffering produces perseverance; perseverance, character; and character, hope. And hope does not disappoint us.

—Romans 5:3-5

"As long as there is breath, there is hope."

That statement has been offered many times as a lifeline of comfort to people in crisis. The underlying premise is true. As long as we are still alive, there is the possibility that circumstances may change. However, I have searched the Scriptures for reasons for hope, and it is never tied to breath or even to change of circumstances. Hope's source is higher than earth and more enduring than time. It is changeless and sure because its foundation is the character of God. Hope challenges us to close our eyes to the circumstances we see and fix with eyes of faith on the great unseen. The path of hope—suffering, perseverance, and character (Rom. 5:3-5), seems so utterly opposite to our expectation. It is like taking a *down* escalator to go *up*. While my nature vehemently resists this path, if I must go down (and life will surely take me there), thank God that the end destination is up. That is hope.

Father, I think of deployed soldiers and their families who have hit the end of hope. I pray for soldiers who have come back broken and for shattered families. The stresses are greater than their capacity to endure. All hope seems extinguished, and yet they still breathe. Throw them the lifeline of hope that will anchor their souls, firm and secure, hope born of him who is Lord over circumstances, hope that will not disappoint. Renew their strength that they may soar like eagles once again. Give them eyes capable of beholding the great unseen. May hope in you encourage them and inspire endurance. Give them the courage to remain on the *down* escalator until it delivers them to the highest floor—the floor of eternal hope.

In the name of Jesus, our blessed hope, Amen.

My hope is built on nothing less
Than Jesus' blood and righteousness;
I dare not trust the sweetest frame,
But wholly lean on Jesus' name.

When darkness veils His lovely face,
I rest on His unchanging grace;
In every high and stormy gale,
My anchor holds within the vale.

HOPE

Refrain
On Christ, the solid rock, I stand;
All other ground is sinking sand,
All other ground is sinking sand.

—From Edward Mote's hymn, "The Solid Rock"

—

EMOTIONS

Jesus wept.

—John 11:35

Then he said to them, "My soul is overwhelmed with sorrow to the point of death."

—Matthew 26:38

"You snakes! You brood of vipers!"

—Jesus' words to the religious establishment in Matthew 23:33

And being in anguish, he prayed more earnestly, and his sweat was like drops of blood falling to the ground.

—Luke 22:44

Then the high priest stood up and said to Jesus, "Are you not going to answer?" . . . But Jesus remained silent.

—Matthew 26:62-63

I know little about military life except what filters through the media and movies. One impression that probably rings true is that the training is harsh and unrelenting. Bodies and minds are pushed to the limits to prepare for that moment when simulation becomes reality. When crisis situations do not allow time for deductive thought and analysis, survival demands instantaneous and instinctive responses. As a soldier's mom, I take comfort in knowing that my son is as prepared as possible for whatever may come. Still, I worry about his humanity. Part of our uniqueness as human beings is our capacity to feel and express emotion. Jesus expressed a wide range of emotions openly, yet he kept his silence before the high priest who sought his death. He did not deny his humanity, but he did not let emotion rule in the moment of crisis. The Psalms, many of which came from the lips of David, one of the greatest warriors of his time, catalog more passionate emotions than any other book in the Bible.

Father, I pray for soldiers to find that balance between accepting and expressing their humanity and not letting emotions rule their perceptions and judgments. May they find an outlet in crying out to you as David and Jesus did, rather than bottling up poisonous feelings inside. Do not let war strip them of their humanity and turn them into passionless mannequins or cold statues. Provide skilled chaplains and counselors to help them with the weights that press on their souls. They will come home to families who relate with them on emotional levels. Do not let them lose what is most precious about them. Help them with this difficult transition when they do come home.

Thank you, Lord, for validating our emotions when you so freely expressed your own.

In Jesus' name, Amen.

TIME

Remember how fleeting is my life.

—Psalm 89:47

My times are in your hands.

—Psalm 31:15

THERE IS A right time for everything: . . . A time for war; A time for peace. What does one really get from hard work? I have thought about this in connection with all the various kinds of work God has given to mankind. Everything is appropriate in its own time. But though God has planted eternity in the hearts of men, even so, man cannot see the whole scope of God's work from beginning to end.

—Ecclesiastes 3:1, 8, 9-11, The Living Bible

I know that there is nothing better for men than to be happy and do good while they live. That everyone may eat and drink, and find satisfaction in all his toil—this is the gift of God.

—Ecclesiastes 3:12-13

Be wise: make the most of every opportunity you have for doing good.

—Ephesians 5:16, The Living Bible

If you have ever known a season, or even a night, of insomnia, you have personal knowledge of the tyranny of time. The second hand marches mercilessly around the clock, unmoved by the anxiety you feel over the sleep you are missing and the demands of tomorrow that you will be ill-equipped to face. In seasons of deep sorrow and pain, time is like the prison guard that will not grant your release until the appointed sentence is served. In moments of sweet joy, time takes wings and flies like a bird in swift flight, and we can only longingly watch it disappear. Time has oppressed us all—even more so for soldiers on deployment and their families.

Father, I pray that the long and difficult days and months will not wear away at the soldiers' souls and cause them to lose heart. You created man and set him in a framework of linear time for your own good purposes. Help us to view time from your perspective.

Help soldiers and families to view seconds and hours as gifts of life, classrooms of learning, and soil for growing. May the awareness of your presence make the time easier to bear. May the fleeting nature of life make each day seem precious. Help them view this time as their appointed season to serve their country faithfully. For all those moments that are too painful for human eyes to see any possible good, grant them the strength to endure, and the ability to trust in your sovereignty and goodness.

In the name of Jesus, Amen.

FRIENDSHIP

Two are better than one, because they have a good return for their work: If one falls down, his friend can help him up. But pity the man who falls and has no one to help him up!

—Ecclesiastes 4:9-10

A friend loves at all times, and a brother is born for adversity.

—Proverbs 17:17

. . . But there is a friend who sticks closer than a brother.

—Proverbs 18:24

"I no longer call you servants. . . I have called you friends."

—Jesus' words to his disciples in John 15:15

"Never will I leave you; never will I forsake you."

—Hebrews 13:5

We can have everything in the world that power and money can obtain, but without a friend to share it with, it is unspeakably empty. In contrast, we can know the depths of poverty or the challenge of adversity but feel extremely rich in the companionship of a true and faithful friend. Never is friendship more critical or more proven than in the time of adversity. A friend is often the determining factor in whether we stand or fall. Have you ever heard these words? "I love you (*friend*) because you are helping me to make of the lumber of my life not a tavern but a temple."[7] What a powerful image!

Friendship can bring something out of us better than we can bring it out ourselves.

Father, I pray for soldiers and their families going through the hardship of deployment and war. Bless them with the gift of good friends who will stand with them in this time of testing and bring them through it more honorably than they can bring themselves through it. I pray for friends with whom they can pour out the contents of their hearts, knowing that gentle ears will receive them without judgment. Let no son, daughter, husband, wife, parent, child, brother, or sister face the anxieties of deployment and war without the shelter of a friend. Thank you that, even if earthly friends fail, we have a friend in Christ, who will never desert.

In Jesus' name, Amen.

RESPECTFUL

Though I am free and belong to no man, I make myself a slave to everyone, to win as many as possible. To the Jews I became like a Jew, to win the Jews. To those under the law I became like one under the law (though I myself am not under the law), so as to win those under the law. . . . To the weak I became weak, to win the weak. I have become all things to all men so that by all possible means I might save some.

—1 Corinthians 9:19-20, 22

Show proper respect to everyone.

—1 Peter 2:17

Make it your ambition to lead a quiet life, to mind your own business and to work with your hands, just as we told you, so that your daily life may win the respect of outsiders.

—1 Thessalonians 4:11-12

"But I tell you: Love your enemies and pray for those who persecute you, that you may be sons of your Father in heaven. He causes his sun to rise on the evil and the good, and sends rain on the righteous and the unrighteous."

—Matthew 5:44-45

Turn on the evening news or pick up a newspaper, and one sickening impression that will stick with you is the little regard that people have for human life. With no apparent regret or remorse, desires and impulses are carried out without the restraining influence of conscience or consequence. If that is so on the streets of our own cities among fellow countrymen, what is it like to be deployed across the world in war situations, where the distinction between enemies and allies is so unclear?

Father, I pray for soldiers to hold on to faith and good conscience, remembering that all men bear the image of God who has given life to all. As they live and work and fight among cultures that are so foreign and counter to their own, help soldiers conduct their day-to-day lives in a way that will honor you and build bridges of trust and respect. Help them see the people through the lens of their own world rather than ours and leave judgments to God.

Give them the heart of the apostle Paul, who was willing to become like the people to whom he ministered so as not to offend them or become a stumbling block to them in any way. Compel soldiers to pray for divine discernment as they interact with the people. You alone, O God, can sort out the moral dilemmas of war and justice and the sacredness of life. Even among the troops themselves, may living a quiet life, minding their own business, doing the work given them to do, and showing respect to everyone be the code of conduct by which each soldier lives.

In the name of Jesus, who became like us (except in sin) that he might save us, Amen.

BROKEN

He heals the brokenhearted and binds up their wounds.

—Psalm 147:3

A bruised reed he will not break, and a smoldering wick he will not snuff out.

—Isaiah 42:3

He has sent me to bind up the brokenhearted, to proclaim freedom for the captives and release from darkness for the prisoners . . . to comfort all who mourn . . . to bestow on them a crown of beauty instead of ashes, the oil of gladness instead of mourning, and a garment of praise instead of a spirit of despair.

—Isaiah 61:1-3

Then he [Jesus] said to them [disciples], "My soul is over-whelmed with sorrow to the point of death. Stay here and keep watch with me."

—Matthew 26:38

A soldier leaves for deployment traveling light, bringing body, soul, spirit, and whatever else he or she can fit into a duffel bag along with standard military issue items. Some return with less, having lost limbs, senses, functional abilities, and spirit. Others return with considerably more—burdens of guilt, paralyzing anxieties, fears, depression, and haunting memories.

Whatever the case, all of them return changed in some way. And sometimes, the life they left behind has changed beyond recognition. Homecoming brings its own set of challenges.

Father, our prayers go up for the men and women returning broken in body, mind, and spirit—for soldiers returning to homes that have changed while they were away. Draw near to the wounded and despairing. Bind up their wounds supernaturally or through skilled and compassionate caregivers. Release them from the dark prisons of guilt, fear, anxiety, memory, and regret. Comfort those who mourn deep loss. Tenderly guard those who have been reduced to *smoldering wicks*, and fan them back to life again. Walk with them as the *Man of Sorrows* who understands better than any other the crushing weight of sorrow that overwhelms the soul. Bring people to their sides who will stay with them and watch with them for as long as they are needed. Give families special grace as they rebuild their lives from broken pieces. Take what seems like shattered glass and fashion from it a mosaic with a beauty of its own.

In Jesus' name, Amen.

RESPONSIBLE

For when one says, "I follow Paul," and another, "I follow Apollos," are you not mere men? What, after all, is Apollos? And what is Paul? Only servants, through whom you came to believe—as the Lord has assigned to each his task. I planted the seed, Apollos watered it, but God made it grow.

—1 Corinthians 3:4-6

"Take my yoke upon you and learn from me, for I am gentle and humble in heart, and you will find rest for your souls. For my yoke is easy and my burden is light."

—Matthew 11:29-30

As I reflect back on life to the responsibilities I have carried—jobs, parenting, marriage, and so on, I know that my intent was always to do my best to fulfill those responsibilities successfully. Responsibility, however, carried with it a certain sense of burden related to the outcome. What if I failed? Sometimes I did.

Father, I think of soldiers on deployment. What a great burden of responsibility there is in keeping the homeland safe, engaging in actions that will change the course of another nation, holding the destiny of other human lives in your hands, and honoring the sacrifice of others who have gone before. I pray they will live with great integrity and accountability, but I also pray they will not carry a burden of responsibility they were never meant to carry.

In *The Shack,* a best selling novel by William Paul Young, there is an interchange between a grief stricken man and the Holy Spirit. The Holy Spirit explains that God's plan was that man would *respond* to life through his indwelling, enabling power, and *life* would be a verb—one that was dynamic and full of possibilities. Man has made the verb a noun, similar to *responsibility,* and life has become a set of rules and obligations, full of fear and failure with God absent from the equation. Perhaps there is more truth to this fictional explanation than we know. What we do know from the above Scriptures is that we each have a part to play, but the final outcome is in God's hand. God desires us to share the *yoke of life* with him. When we do, the burden is light.

Father, give soldiers the capacity to see and trust that a greater hand is guiding eternal outcomes. Help them respond to each situation with expectancy that you are there beside them. Free them from burdens of responsibility that were never meant to be carried alone. Let soldiers do the tasks given them to do faithfully and diligently. Then help them let go and realize that they have fulfilled their service. The outcome is in the hands of God, who holds the power to work all things for good.

In the name of the one whose burden is light, Amen.

FORGIVENESS

For all have sinned and fall short of the glory of God.
>—Romans 3:23

Therefore, there is now no condemnation for those who are in Christ Jesus.
>—Romans 8:1

If we confess our sins, he is faithful and just and will forgive us our sins and purify us from all unrighteousness.
>—1 John 1:9

He [God] does not treat us as our sins deserve or repay us according to our iniquities. For as high as the heavens are above the earth, so great is his love for those who fear him; as far as the east is from the west, so far has he removed our transgressions from us.
>—Psalm 103:10-12

The Spirit of the Sovereign LORD is on me, because the LORD has anointed me to preach good news to the poor. He has sent me to bind up the brokenhearted, to proclaim freedom for the captives and release from darkness for the prisoners.
>—Isaiah 61:1

To live is to need forgiveness. Guilt is perhaps one of the darkest enemies a soldier can encounter. Fighting on the battle-field of the heart and mind, this Enemy's weapon is the arsenal of thoughts that come like sniper fire, reminding soldiers of the wrongs they have done—how they have taken life, taken down the innocent with the guilty, lived when a comrade has died, made decisions that proved costly, given in to temptation, and been absent when family needed them. This endless volley specifically targets vulnerable spots. Soldiers experiencing this assault are as much prisoners of war as the ones locked away in foreign cells. Often they carry their prisons with them when they return.

Father, make the message of Easter real, personal, and liberating to them today. Enable them to receive the forgiveness you so freely offer and find peace. Allow chaplains and counselors to be agents of grace, leading soldiers to the deep pools of mercy found in your Word. Give them eyes to see that in their guilt they share in the brotherhood of all humanity, for we have all fallen short. Lead them also to the liberty found in extending forgiveness to others so that they will avoid the equally imprisoning enemy of bitterness.

I pray for grace and forgiveness to flow freely in families that have incurred deep hurt as a consequence of deployment. Let today be the day of release for many who have lived too long in captivity to guilt or anger.

Thank you for being a God of tender mercy and forgiveness, always waiting with open arms.

In the name of Jesus, whose mission was to set the captives free, Amen.

PERSEVERANCE

I have fought the good fight, I have finished the race, I have kept the faith.

—2 Timothy 4:7

But one thing I do: Forgetting what is behind and straining toward what is ahead, I press on toward the goal.

—Philippians 3:13-14

. . . And let us run with perseverance the race marked out for us.

—Hebrews 12:1

Let us not become weary in doing good, for at the proper time we will reap a harvest if we do not give up.

—Galatians 6:9

At the sound of the starting signal, runners from all over the world will test their perseverance as the Boston Marathon kicks off this week. Unlike recreational running, a marathon requires serious preparation, discipline, and determination to finish the course. So much of life is like a marathon. We cannot be unprepared. Hard stretches will demand everything we have to give and more.

I recently stumbled upon a Web site that offers advice on how to prepare for marathon running. Some of the strategies and prerequisites seemed generic for life: the importance of motivation and self-discipline, keeping your self-talk positive, expecting times of adversity and being mentally prepared for the challenges ahead, running in a group for encouragement, and having a goal. In long runs, persevering through the bad patches of the later miles requires mental toughness to push through. It strikes me how similar military deployment is to a marathon.

Father, I think of soldiers and their families who find themselves in a place where it is hard to persevere. Help them maintain the motivation and self-discipline to press on to the finish line. Counter defeating thoughts with words of hope and confident determination. When the bad patches come, remind them that they are common to every runner. Give them the mental toughness to push through. Incline them to run in groups, encouraging one another through the rough spots. Keep the vision of the finish line ever before them, and remind them that every step brings them closer to it. Be their strength when they feel like giving up. By your grace, may each soldier finish well. Keep us persevering in prayer for them until you bring them home.

In Jesus' name, Amen.

CHARACTER

A good name is more desirable than great riches; to be esteemed is better than silver or gold.

—Proverbs 22:1

A good name is better than fine perfume.

—Ecclesiastes 7:1

Ascribe to the LORD the glory due his name.

—Psalm 29:2

You shall not misuse the name of the LORD your God, for the LORD will not hold anyone guiltless who misuses his name.

—Exodus 20:7

Therefore God exalted him [Christ] to the highest place and gave him the name that is above every name.

—Philippians 2:9

Not only so, but we also rejoice in our sufferings, because we know that suffering produces perseverance; perseverance, character; and character, hope.

—Romans 5:3-4

Just in our lifetime, technology has completely changed the landscape of our lives. The implements and techniques of modern warfare would look very foreign to soldiers of previous generations. One thing, though, has changed very little—the soldier's dog tags. Every soldier wears around his or her neck the essential information that identifies them. A soldier's name, however, represents so much more than the raised letters on a tiny piece of metal. A person's name represents their essential nature—the unique set of qualities and ethical traits that define who they are and how they live. We know from Scripture the supreme value God has placed on his name and character. He exhorts us to do the same. A good name, reputation, and character are of greater worth than earth's treasures. There is also the Scriptural connection between suffering (adversity) and character. It is not that we should like pain or deny its tragedy, but we should ask God to use the difficulties of life to build character.

Father, our soldiers (and their families) face adversity with every sunrise. I pray that you would bless every struggle to the building of good character so that they may come home richer than they left. As the refiner of ores carefully controls the heat and closely watches until he can see his reflection in the metal, stay close to each soldier through the fiery trials. May your image become more and more visible in them. Remind them that no compromise is more costly than a compromise of character. Whatever losses soldiers may have to face, I pray they will only know gain in character.

To the one whose name is above every other name I pray, Amen.

> For every hill I've had to climb,
> For every stone that bruised my feet,
> For all the blood and sweat and grime,
> For blinding storms and burning heat,
> My heart sings but a grateful song—
> These were the things that made me strong.

CHARACTER

For all the heartaches and the tears,
For all the anguish and the pain,
For gloomy days and fruitless years,
And for the hopes that lived in vain,
I do give thanks, for now I know
These were the things that helped me grow!

—Anonymous
quoted by Mrs. Charles Cowan in *Streams in the Desert*[8]

VIGILANCE

Be sober, be vigilant; because your adversary the devil walks about like a roaring lion, seeking whom he may devour.

—1 Peter 5:8 NKJV

Be very careful, then, how you live—not as unwise but as wise, making the most of every opportunity, because the days are evil.

—Ephesians 5:15-16

. . . For Satan himself masquerades as an angel of light.

—2 Corinthians 11:14

My help comes from the LORD, the Maker of heaven and earth. He will not let your foot slip—he who watches over you will not slumber. . . . The LORD will watch over your coming and going both now and forevermore.

—Psalm 121:2, 3, 8

With all the trees and flowers bursting forth, we realize what a wonderful gift color is. In our time, however, color has taken on an additional and more ominous association. Today, red, orange, yellow, blue, and green designate levels of alertness to potential threats to our nation and set in motion a cascade of actions to avert potential tragedies.

Evil has always been a threat, but today's technologies and accessibility of information have put weapons in the arsenal of evil, making it more difficult to detect and combat than ever before. The enemy is not always easy to spot. He or she often looks harmless. For soldiers, it is a little like being in a house of mirrors. It is hard to tell which image is the real thing. Living in a world of escalating evil requires constant vigilance.

Vigilance is a demanding state of being. It is difficult to maintain without drifting into paranoia, unable to trust anyone, or being lulled into a state of laxity by uneventful periods of calm. Soldiers must somehow find the balance.

Father, give soldiers a spirit of discernment to recognize true evil. May it become their habitual practice to pray for divine guidance. Give them the strength, endurance, and clarity of mind to maintain the posture of constant alertness. When they are stretched to their human limits and find it difficult to remain alert, be their shield and protector. During periods of apparent calm, help soldiers remember that evil only pauses to regroup. Keep them from being deceived into letting down their guard.

Father, we believe there is great power in prayer. Help us be vigilant in prayer for our soldiers. May our prayers cover them when evil presses in.

In Jesus' name, Amen.

INSUFFICIENT

They reeled and staggered like drunken men; they were at their wits' end. Then they cried out to the LORD in their trouble, and He brought them out of their distress.

—Psalm 107:27-28

And a woman was there who had been subject to bleeding for twelve years. She had suffered a great deal under the care of many doctors and had spent all she had. . . . When she heard about Jesus, she came up behind him in the crowd and touched his cloak because she thought, "If I just touch his clothes, I will be healed." . . . At once Jesus realized that power had gone out from him.

—Mark 5:25-28, 30

But he said to me, "My grace is sufficient for you, for my power is made perfect in weakness." . . . For when I am weak, then I am strong.

—2 Corinthians 12:9, 10

Not that we are sufficient of ourselves to think of anything as being from ourselves, but our sufficiency is from God.

—2 Corinthians 3:5 NKJV

One of the most difficult times for the human ego is when we come up against something we cannot do—when we are completely spent physically, emotionally, financially, and intellectually, and we are at the end of ourselves. We are raised to believe we can do anything we put our minds to. Sooner or later, life will expose our insufficiencies, pressing us to the place where we have nothing left to give. How we despise this place that looks so hopeless and feels so defeating. When we face our insufficiencies, however, God shows us his complete sufficiency.

Soldiers are taught to be strong and to never give up or give in. Merciful God, when soldiers hit the wall and reach the outer limits of human ability, step in with your all-sufficient power. Families back home have pressures of their own that leave them *spent*. May soldiers and families dare to reach out and touch you, Lord. When they do, let your power instantly flow into them. Make these moments of weakness become moments of great strength, because the strength is yours. Remind them that you never expect them to be more than you created them to be—human, with human limitations. Meet them when they are at their wit's end and deliver them from their distress.

In Jesus' name, Amen.

Are you standing at "Wit's End Corner,"
Christian, with troubled brow?
Are you thinking of what is before you,
And all you are bearing now?
Does all the world seem against you,
And you in the battle alone?
Remember—at "Wit's End Corner,"
Is just where God's power is shown.

Are you standing at "Wit's End Corner,"
Blinded with wearying pain,
Feeling you cannot endure it,
You cannot bear the strain,
Bruised through the constant suffering,
Dizzy, and dazed, and numb?
Remember—at "Wit's End Corner"
Is where Jesus loves to come.

INSUFFICIENT

Are you standing at "Wit's End Corner"?
Your work before you spread,
All lying begun, unfinished,
And pressing on heart and head,
Longing for strength to do it,
Stretching out trembling hands?
Remember—at "Wit's End Corner"
The Burden-bearer stands.

Are you standing at "Wit's End Corner"?
Then you're just in the very spot
To learn the wondrous resources
Of Him who faileth not.
No doubt to a brighter pathway
Your footsteps will soon be moved,
But only at "Wit's End Corner"
Is the "God who is able" proved.

—Antoinette Wilson[9]

ANGER

"Therefore I will not keep silent; I will speak out in the anguish of my spirit. I will complain in the bitterness of my soul. . . . Let me alone. . . . What is man that you make so much of him, that you give him so much attention, that you examine him every morning and test him every moment? . . . Why have you made me your target?"

—Job 7:11, 16-18, 20

Why, O LORD, do you stand far off? Why do you hide yourself in times of trouble?

—Psalm 10:1

Everyone should be quick to listen, slow to speak and slow to become angry, for man's anger does not bring about the righteous life that God desires.

—James 1:19-20

For our struggle is not against flesh and blood, but against the rulers, against the authorities, against the powers of this dark world and against the spiritual forces of evil in the heavenly realms.

—Ephesians 6: 12

"The LORD is slow to anger. . . ."

—Numbers 14:18

Jesus said, "Father, forgive them, for they do not know what they are doing."

—Luke 23:34

Emotions are powerful things. They can carry us to the mountaintops or cast us to the depths of despair. They can propel us to world-impacting accomplishments or, if undisciplined, they can land us in big trouble. Just as physical pain is a warning sign that something is wrong with bodies, emotions deserve our attention and intervention. The physical and emotional are closely linked. When we are physically depleted by fatigue, stress, anxiety, and illness, the scale seems to tip, and emotions rule. Military deployment provides fertile soil for emotions to grow out of control—especially anger. For soldiers, anger at comrades who annoy, commanders who expect the impossible, government that has not provided the support needed, enemies who stalk like wolves in sheep's clothing, and family members at home who need things they are unable to give, all compound like interest on a credit card. Families back home deal with issues of feeling abandoned to face life's pressures alone, raising kids, facing financial hardships, and having to make decisions for which they will likely be criticized. They are facing things they never signed on to face.

Father God, thank you that Scripture records the example of people who felt the fires of anger and poured out their complaints to you. It is part of the human experience. Humans, however, are rarely right in their assessment of the source of anger, often detonating its explosive power on the wrong target. If we are honest, our target is often you, Lord.

Thank you for showing us the high and low roads of anger and for teaching us what to strive for and what to avoid. Creator of feelings, be master of them when soldiers and families are most vulnerable. May your restraining power flow through them. Like Job and King David, may soldiers lay out their complaints and pour out their raw emotions before you where the destructive energy can be defused and the light of truth applied. You did not condemn Job when he questioned and accused you, succumbed to self-pity and engaged in a war of sarcastic words. Kept inside, those feelings would have been more lethal than the sores covering his body. Instead, you revealed yourself to him, and that was sufficient to silence his anger. Reveal yourself again when soldiers and families battle anger. Remind them that judgment belongs to God alone, and though it may be delayed, justice will be accomplished. Let the mercy you have shown them make them ready to show mercy to others. Help them choose the high road of forgiveness and turn their anger toward the real enemy—evil.

In Jesus' name, Amen.

GRATITUDE

Give everyone what you owe him: If you owe taxes, pay taxes; if revenue, then revenue; if respect, then respect; if honor, then honor.

—Romans 13:7

If one part suffers, every part suffers with it; if one part is honored, every part rejoices with it.

—1 Corinthians 12:26

"Greater love has no one than this, that he lay down his life for his friends."

—John 15:13

O beautiful for heroes proved in liberating strife,
Who more than self their country loved,
And mercy more than life!
America, America, May God thy gold refine
Till all success be nobleness
And every gain divine!

—"America the Beautiful"

Praise the Power that hath made and preserved us a nation!
Then conquer we must, when our cause it is just;
And this be our motto: "In God is our trust!"
And the Star Spangled Banner in triumph shall wave
O'er the land of the free, and the home of the brave.

—"The Star Spangled Banner"

We remember the lyrics to our patriot songs even when we are unable to retrieve much of the other information stored in the vast data banks of our minds. Perhaps this is because they are stored in our hearts as well as our minds. We are stirred by these songs because they remind us of our blessings and call us to reflect on the inestimable cost of war—the cost of sons, daughters, moms, dads, brothers, sisters, grandpas, grandmas, aunts, uncles, and friends—*heroes proved in liberating strife, who more than self their country loved, and mercy more than life!* They are America's gold, refined in the fires of war. It is because of their sacrifice that we can sing. We honor them once again this Memorial Day.

Father, bless and comfort families whose devastating losses have been freedom's gain. Heal the piercing wounds of war as only you can. We give them what we owe—our deepest gratitude for laying down their lives for us. In doing so, they have demonstrated the highest love. Help us find practical ways to express our gratitude. May we draw close enough to feel the suffering of those who have suffered and rejoice at the opportunity to honor them. For those who are currently serving, we lift up our most heartfelt prayers for divine blessing, protection, and provision. Hide them beneath the shelter of your great wings and guard them in all their ways. Bless their families who share the sacrifice.

We acknowledge and give thanks to you for you are *the Power that made and preserved us a nation!* May we never be so foolish as to forsake our motto: *In God is our trust!*

In Jesus' name, Amen.

FOCUSED

During the fourth watch of the night Jesus went out to them, walking on the lake. When the disciples saw him walking on the lake, they were terrified. . . ."Lord, if it's you," Peter replied, "tell me to come to you on the water." "Come," he said. Then Peter got down out of the boat, walked on the water and came toward Jesus. But when he saw the wind, he was afraid and, beginning to sink, cried out, "Lord, save me!"

—Matthew 14:25-26, 28-30

"Therefore do not worry about tomorrow, for tomorrow will worry about itself. Each day has enough trouble of its own."

—Matthew 6:34

In an earlier devotional, we considered the importance of perspective, acknowledging that we see through our limited lens of humanity a tiny portion of the larger picture of life. We react and make judgments based on our limited perspective. Often these interpretations prove wrong once we get to see more and more of the larger picture. We have to trust the One who sees the whole picture. There is, perhaps, a companion truth to this—the importance of focus. For reasons we do not comprehend, the eternal God created us to live within the boundaries of time. Life is given to us in moments. We cannot know or control the number of them. Like currency, we can only decide how we spend them. While *perspective* tells us there is a larger picture that we are not yet privileged to see, *focus* tells us to use wisely the present moment we do see.

The above story from the book of Matthew of Peter walking on water toward Jesus illustrates the important lesson of focus. The moment we take our eyes off of our destination and begin looking at the wider threatening circumstances around us, we falter and sink. How difficult yet critical this must be for soldiers and their families! It is a foundational mindset for soldiers if they are to accomplish their mission and not sink. It is just as critical for families to focus on the challenge of the moment and not borrow tomorrow's trouble.

Father, help soldiers to stay focused on the moment at hand, which is all they have to *spend*. The moment their minds begin to widen and focus on fearful, doubting, dark places, bring them back to the task at hand. If they should begin to sink, reach out your hand and draw them back up. Turn their eyes toward the One who holds power over circumstances—the One who has overcome evil and knows the path to victory. Keep them alert to present danger and opportunities. Give them strength and courage for the challenges of each moment. Comfort them with the thought that you are the God of moments, present in each one to bless and supply.

In Jesus' name, Amen.

HOMECOMING

. . . Ahab went to meet Elijah. When he saw Elijah, he said to him, "Is that you, you troubler of Israel?" "I have not made trouble for Israel," Elijah replied. "But you and your father's family have. You have abandoned the LORD's commands and have followed the Baals. Now summon the people from all over Israel to meet me on Mount Carmel. And bring the four hundred and fifty prophets of Baal and the four hundred prophets of Asherah. . . . Get two bulls for us. Let them choose one for themselves, and let them cut it into pieces and put it on the wood but not set fire to it. I will prepare the other bull. . . . Then you call on the name of your god, and I will call on the name of the LORD. The god who answers by fire—he is God." . . . They [the prophets of Baal] continued their frantic prophesying until the time for the evening sacrifice. But there was no response. . . . The prophet Elijah stepped forward and prayed. . . . Then the fire of the LORD fell and burned up the sacrifice, the wood, the stones and the soil, and also licked up the water in the trench. [Then the king's wife Jezebel threatened to kill Elijah.] . . . Elijah was afraid and ran for his life. . . . He came to a broom tree, sat down under it and prayed that he might die. "I have had enough, LORD," he said. "Take my life; I am no better than my ancestors." Then he lay down under the tree and fell asleep.

—1 Kings 18:16-19, 23-24, 29, 36, 38, 19:3-5

The finish line that always seemed so far away is now in sight. The deployment is almost over. Visions of homecoming are now permitted into one's thoughts. I have tried to imagine what that moment would be like for soldiers and families. Before packing that moment with many expectations, the analogy of finishing a race reins me in.

Marathon runners breaking through the finish line usually collapse, completely spent. They hunger for air, lack energy, and suffer significant pain from the extreme demands placed on their bodies for such a long period of time. Can it be any different for soldiers? The prophet Elijah, after a stunning but emotionally draining victory over the hundreds of false prophets, experienced such complete fatigue and discouragement that he wanted to die. But God cared for his physical needs, with rest and food delivered by unusual means—the birds.

Father, I pray for soldiers returning home, completely depleted and numbed by experiences more difficult than they could ever have imagined, with nervous systems so revved up from prolonged stress and extraordinary responsibility that they cannot calm down and smoothly fit into a totally different set of demands. Divinely intervene to provide the period of rest and recuperation they need. Enable family members who are also depleted to extend grace and understanding. Help soldiers with the enormous emotional adjustment of changing worlds in the span of an airplane flight. Smooth the transition back into family life after having missed a whole chapter of the story.

I pray for both soldiers and families to filter every thought and emotion through the lens of gratitude—for life spared, mutual sacrifices made, freedoms and blessings enjoyed, and for the opportunity to serve. Bless each returning soldier, each family member who shared the sacrifice, and each person who offered support through prayer, gifts, practical help, and friendship. Be with all those who are now picking up the baton and continuing the race where these faithful ones have left off. Graciously lead them through the difficult journey ahead.

In Jesus' name, Amen.

THANKSGIVING

Now on his way to Jerusalem, Jesus traveled along the border between Samaria and Galilee. As he was going into a village, ten men who had leprosy met him. They stood at a distance and called out in a loud voice, "Jesus, Master, have pity on us!" When he saw them, he said, "Go show yourselves to the priests." And as they went, they were cleansed. One of them, when he saw he was healed, came back, praising God in a loud voice. He threw himself at Jesus' feet and thanked him—and he was a Samaritan. Jesus asked, "Were not all ten cleansed? Where are the other nine? Was no one found to return and give praise to God except this foreigner?" Then he said to him, "Rise and go; your faith has made you well."

—Luke 17:11-19

In Jesus' day, to contract leprosy was to receive a death sentence—whether to die literally from injury and infection or know the living death of separation and isolation from society required by the disease. The ten leprous men in the story from the book of Luke cried out to Jesus for help. They had some measure of faith that he could help them or they would not have bothered to ask. Jesus did not let them down. He instructed them to go and show themselves to the priests so they could be reinstated into society. They were healed as they went.

In a sense, we have relived their story. Over the past year, we have dared to go to Jesus to ask him to spare life, show mercy, and help our soldier loved ones deployed in dangerous places, who are living the experience of isolation and separation on a daily basis. We have gathered our measure of faith and offered up our prayers to the One who is able and willing to answer. God did not disappoint us. Now let us be like the one leper who returned to give thanks and praise.

Thank you, God, for hearing our prayers. Thank you for every soldier who has returned safely home. Thank you for sustaining families through the long deployment separation. For all that you have enabled soldiers to endure and accomplish, we give thanks. For every person who can now know a greater measure of hope and freedom because of sacrifices that have been made, we offer thanks. For the blessings of strength and character that cost so dearly, blessings we would never have dared to choose on our own, we give thanks.

I am not sure why the other nine lepers in the story failed to return to thank Jesus for making them whole. I am guessing, however, that the one who ran back to express gratitude lived a richer life because he recognized the supreme value of what he had been given. May we choose the path of gratitude he chose and experience the richness of life that is the fruit of a thankful heart.

In Jesus' name, Amen.

ENDNOTES

1. Stephen Mansfield, *The Faith of the American Soldier* (New York: Jeremy P. Tarcher / Penguin, 2005), 8.

2. Max Lucado, *3:16 The Numbers Of Hope* (Nashville: Thomas Nelson, 2007), 170.

3. Ken Gire, *Reflections on the Word* (Colorado Springs: Chariot Victor Publishing, 1998), 82-83.

4. Ibid., 83.

5. Mrs. Charles Cowman, *Streams in the Desert, Volume 2,* (Grand Rapids, MI: Zondervan Publishing House, Daybreak Books, 1966), 47.

6. Mrs. Charles Cowman, *Streams in the Desert* (Grand Rapids, MI: Zondervan Publishing House, a Cowman Publication, 1965), 19.

7. These lines are often attributed to Roy Croft. One book in which they appear is *The Language of Friendship* (Boulder, CO: Blue Mountain Press, 1999), but they also appear in various Internet sites and finding the original author is problematic.

8. Cowman, *Streams in the Desert, Volume 2,* Daybreak Books edition, 167.

9. Cowman, *Streams in the Desert*, a Cowman Publication, 155.

CPSIA information can be obtained at www.ICGtesting.com
Printed in the USA
LVOW081133030413

327365LV00001B/91/P